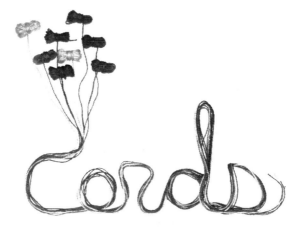

Cords

Reflections on Weaving
the Tapestry of Life

Patricia Tibbs

TATE PUBLISHING & ENTERPRISES

The opinions expressed by the author are not necessarily those of Tate Publishing, LLC.

Published by Tate Publishing & Enterprises, LLC
127 E. Trade Center Terrace | Mustang, Oklahoma 73064 USA
1.888.361.9473 | www.tatepublishing.com

Tate Publishing is committed to excellence in the publishing industry. The company reflects the philosophy established by the founders, based on Psalm 68:11,
"The Lord gave the word and great was the company of those who published it."

Published in the United States of America

ISBN: 978-1-61777-605-2
Biography & Autobiography / Cultural Heritage
11.08.30

To Anyu,
Thank you, the memories are sweet.
And Apuka

Acknowledgments

I want to thank Patrick and my children for loving me. I also want to thank my brothers and sisters for being who they are. I especially want to thank Tate Publishing for making it all happen.

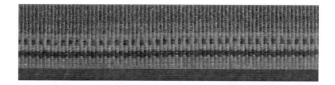

Table of Contents

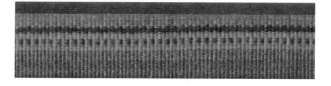

Introduction

I once had a fascinating conversation with one of my colleagues. He has taken several mission trips to Africa, specifically to Kenya. He has enjoyed these trips immensely, but during the conversation he made a comment that he could not understand why there was all this tribal warfare when they (the Kenyans) were all the same. I looked at this white, very Southern friend of mine and had a good long laugh.

I proceeded to describe to him how different the people in each tribe are. They look different, and they all speak differently. He was amazed. It occurred to me then that it appears to be the nature of human beings to draw lines about them based on difference. I never understood what racism really was until I came to the United States. But I knew exactly what tribalism was. It is a problem in most of Africa, and Uganda has not been spared. Uganda, with its population of approximately thirty-one million in 2007, has over twenty different tribes. This conversation began my reflections on a life that is unique because I have never quite fit into any one group. In Uganda, no one could guess my tribe, unless they were told. Through the years, I have been called various colors depending on where I am. It always seemed important to people to put me into a category. It has never really bothered me and I have never really dwelt on the issue of race too much.

So for me to be writing a book about race when I have spent my whole life not paying much attention to it is a unique experience. As recently as forty years ago, mixed marriages were not common. They were not only frowned upon, but some had dire consequences as a brief survey of the literature will immediately reveal. By mixed marriages, I am not referring to just race, but countries of origin, tribes, castes, and the list goes on—Jews and non-Jews, Italians and Irish, Southerners and Yankees,

PATRICIA TIBBS

Baganda and Acholis, Tutsis and Huttus, the different castes in India, blacks and whites.

The human landscape has changed dramatically.

More and more people have such a unique heritage that putting them into one category is a stretch. I laughed when I heard how Tiger Woods describes himself: "Cablanasian!" A word that does seem to capture his whole heritage.

This book is a memoir of my experiences in the various categories of race. Unlike some who have changed their identity to pass as one race or another, I have always been me. The only difference has been other people's perception of who they think I am based on their frame of reference.

The chapters are the various colors and start with a recent event that triggered the thought followed by a story in my life that describes how it played out. Some of the stories have been changed a little—not because I do not remember the details, but to allow the people involved to tell their own story if they ever choose to. This is not a historical text, nor is it a source of official data. It is a story. It is a tale of experiences in the context of historical events that were on going with many other stories in them. Any numbers quoted are only estimates that I heard over the course of my experiences, but they are not likely to be too far off the mark. Any opinions expressed are mine and are formed from my experiences and my training. Some could be considered expert opinion from a doctor who has practiced many years, others, just the ramblings of a mother who has given opinions to her children for many years. These are probably not far off the mark either. Probably. Intertwined in the narrative is a story of what makes families strong and what should be the focus of our energies instead of our race and the circumstances of our birth.

PATRICIA TIBBS

Black

Know Who You Are

I had heard the question the first time, but I hesitated. I was unsure how to answer. I was amazed to realize that no one had ever asked me that question before. The more I scanned my memory, the more bewildered I became. At twenty-six years of age and living in the latter few years of the twentieth century, no one had ever directly asked me what my race was. Here I was, in a hospital in the suburbs of Chicago, getting ready to have my first child, and I could not even answer a simple question. This did not bode well for what was to come! The nurse continued to look at me with a mildly amused but impatient look.

"We need it to complete the form. We could mark other?"

Now that is interesting.

"What race are you?"

"Other."

It sounded so misplaced, like I did not belong anywhere. Like I belonged in the miscellaneous pile. The place they looked when they had checked everywhere else.

Other.

She was from the "other" clan. Well, that was just it. No one was from the "other" clan. Everybody had a clan. Where I grew up, you took on the clan of your father. Your dad determined where you belonged. There was no half this or half that. No one had a hyphenated name, as if there was a fight between the clans and they all wanted representation. You just belonged to your father. You never married anyone from your clan or there would be serious consequences—consequences that had something to do with being cursed for generations. You also always remembered your mother's clan because you could never marry anyone from that clan either. But you were not your mother's clan.

PATRICIA TIBBS

I looked up at the nurse who was now tapping her pen against her paper. She appeared to know exactly what needed to be written on that piece of paper, but it was not up to her to decide. The fact that she had asked the question, I realized, meant that this was debatable. Well, this I took as an indication that great thought was required on the matter. Why my brain chose that moment to grind to a halt and analyze the situation was interesting because I had spent the preceding nine months doing absolutely nothing that required much thinking. I am sure I have come across at least one study that says pregnancy does not affect one's ability to think, but I could have read that while I was pregnant, which means the study could have said anything.

I was now married and my children would all belong to my husband's clan, but I was still my father's clan: *Ongoda*. That would never change. I was not worried about my children being of my husband's clan because I would always be their mother. Trying to change this tradition was not important to me.

People go against tradition for different reasons. For some, it is an act of rebellion. This is usually such a waste of time. Life is so short. You blink once, and the rainy season is over, you are all grown up, and friends have moved on. You blink twice, and your children have grown up, you are away from home, and the rainy season is no longer part of the calendar. It is now spring when everything is new.

Others go against tradition to make something better. My mind wandered at that moment to my mother. What was it like when she was getting ready to have me, her first born? I had to smile when I thought about that. She would not have had a problem if she were asked this question. In fact, at that time, few people had any problems with this question because it was hardly ever asked. It was almost always obvious where you belonged.

⌘

My mother came home in the spring of 1964 talking about wanting to get married. There was no ring to show for it because that was not done then. My grandmother, Mama, was very excited and wanted to meet the man as soon as possible. She had a lot of questions.

PATRICIA TIBBS

The usual questions.

The ones that are always asked in situations like this. You know, where is he from? What color are his eyes? Is he tall? What does he do? Nothing difficult really. But, for some reason, a difficult-to-explain reason, my mother hesitated. How was she to begin? My grandmother noted the hesitation and began to worry.

My mother was their third daughter; the other two were married to good men. They all farmed the land and lived close by. This daughter was the smartest of them all and was at the university in Szeged, Hungary, studying math. Ilona would be a teacher one day. What an honor. None of the neighbors had children that were smart enough to go to university.

Mama looked out into the courtyard. It was not a large yard, but it was sufficient. The front part of the yard was separated from the back by an eight-foot-high wire mesh fence. The front yard had two buildings apart from the main house. The kitchen was just big enough for the family of six. This was where they cooked and ate. The boiler room was next to it. A furnace that was constantly lit in the winter had been turned off with the onset of milder weather. It would be turned on later when hot water would be needed and supper was started. A well was located in the middle of the front yard. Mama listened to the squeaking of the wheel as my uncle, her only son, turned it. He was collecting water to feed the pigs. In the backyard, Mama's chickens squawked intermittently. A pig grunted and squealed loudly, demanding to be fed. In a little while, the eight pigs in the pen would set up a deafening squealing that would drown out any attempts at conversation for several minutes until they were fed.

Mama waited until the noise died down, leaving only intermittent contented grunts from the pig pen.

"Ilonka, what are you not telling me? Is he a drunkard? You know how hard it is with your father; although, God bless his soul, he does work hard when he is not drunk. Is he German? You know how we feel about those Nazis!"

"He is from Africa." A simple, quiet statement that rocked the world for my grandmother.

She was silent. Her mouth moved, but for a while, nothing would come out.

Even the pigs were quiet. The chickens must have found what it was they were constantly scratching for on the ground. They too were quiet.

Africa? Mama wanted to know what that meant. It was hard for her to sort this out because she had never seen an African. Ever. Having lived since infancy within a ten-mile radius of where they now lived, this news was beyond the scope of her imagination. The small Magyar village on the banks of the Danube River had been big enough for her growing up, and she figured it was just fine for her children too. She had heard of Africans on the radio, the few times they did listen. There had been something in the news about African countries attaining independence. They were not sure what that was, but it always seemed to involve fighting. There was always fighting in Africa whenever they listened. There had been a lot of fighting recently, enough fighting for a lifetime. The war of '39 had left its mark on them all. Grandpa had fought in this war. He never was the same after that. But this was different. Mama had been confident that there would never again be a war in Hungary. I am not sure where she got this confidence from, but she seemed quite certain in her belief. She felt safe where she was, and could not imagine having to worry about war again.

"I thought they were all Negroes in Africa," she eventually managed. There had been something in the news the year before about a Negro who was stirring up trouble in America. He had given a speech of some sort with a humongous crowd in attendance. Even in America, the Negroes were fighting. To her thinking, the only people who were still fighting anywhere were Negroes. She really had no idea what was going on anywhere else in the world, except that now that it had come up, she seemed to recall all this.

"Yes."

"Absolutely not!" Mama sputtered.

"But he is a good man; he is studying to be a doctor. And he loves me."

"Ilonka, my dear Ilona, you have lost your mind. Come home. All that schooling has messed with your mind. You are not thinking clearly. Where will you live? He cannot be a doctor here! No one will go to him. Come home. In time you will meet a good, hardworking Magyar man, and everything will be okay. You do not need that degree."

Mama was pacing up and down, wringing her hands, trying to come up with a solution to this dilemma. "Your father will be home shortly. After he has a good night's rest, he will go to Szeged with you and help you pack up."

"He is coming here to visit in two days."

"He is not welcome!" she screamed. "You do not even know anything about him. He could be… he could be…" She could not think up something dire enough at that point. "You should have asked us first!"

After a prolonged face off, which my uncle watched with some amusement, Mama, seeing such determination on her usually quiet daughter's face, turned away quietly.

"Wait until your father gets here."

Later, a quiet neigh at the gate announced grandpa's arrival. He was thoroughly inebriated and asleep in the wagon. His horse as usual had found the way home. Grandmother helped him down and sent their son to take care of the horse. Grandpa was loud and boisterous.

"Ilonka! What brings you home? Is it summer already? I must be more out of it than I thought! Give your father a kiss!" He tried for a hug, but he ended up losing his balance, going down with a loud laugh. He had a lot of jokes to tell. He was always funny when he was drunk. But Grandmother had had enough.

"Ilona is marrying an African, a Negro."

Loud laughter followed this. "I knew you were special. I knew you were going places. I just knew it. I must be worse than usual because I just heard you were marrying a Negro!" His speech was barely understandable, and after that brilliant statement, he passed out for the night.

Grandpa had a massive headache the next day. Mama told him it served him right, whereupon he went into a long, one-sided dialogue about how he had migraines and would one day die of them and no one cared. He saw my mother then; his changing expressions were a reflection of his feelings as he first showed pleasure at seeing his daughter, then confusion, and finally he shook his head with a troubled expression.

"Did I hear right? Or was it a dream?"

"No dream" she answered quietly, "he is coming to visit in two days."

He looked at his wife, who looked like she had a lot to say on the matter, but she remained quiet. He noted that her eyes were swollen and puffy, something he had not seen in a while since she had gotten used to his drunken returns from work. After she realized that he always came home, and was ready to go back to work the next morning, she had stopped fussing and crying. It had been years. He looked back at his daughter. He would really miss her if she decided to marry this man. He, unlike his wife, my grandmother, had actually met Negroes. And they were people. He searched his daughter's face and saw determination. The same determination that had taken her all the way to Szeged to go to school. Very few of the boys went past high school, and they did not know any other girl who did. He shrugged in resignation. He did have much to say on the subject in subsequent days, but he never told her she could not marry him. My grandmother proceeded to get ready for a wedding with a heavy heart.

⌘

They were married that August in the most memorable wedding that village had ever seen, and has ever seen since. Everybody in the village and for miles around came. Everybody. Everyone who was not nursing a newborn or giving birth to one came. Some who could not walk were conveyed there by various means. Those who had pressing engagements that required their presence at home took shifts to take care of business while they went to witness it. People climbed up on the roof, the walls, on trees, and even on neighboring roofs to witness the proceedings.

The Negro wedding.

Excitement abounded, people talked, danced, and drank, and all were polite and thoroughly enjoyed themselves. Mama was surprised at the response of the people, expecting ridicule, shame, and malicious gossip. But this was so outside everyone's frame of reference that those responses were

PATRICIA TIBBS

not possible. On the outside, Mama was reveling like everyone else.

On the inside, something was dying. It could not have been worse if her daughter had died. Mama consoled herself in the sure hope that this African doctor would soon tire of their daughter and send the girl back. He could keep the children. They would not fit in.

⌘

Two children were born while they were still in Szeged, the first born, a daughter and a son. The son would be the heir to his father's wealth. At the time, this wealth was non-existent, and the family lived sparingly in a small apartment. But sons were very important. They carried on the clan's name. There was a promise of prosperity to come. Daughters were wealth. Good men would pay a large bride price for beautiful, well brought up daughters. Sons were a promise. They ensured that the wealth stayed within the immediate family and did not pass on to a male relative. Sons secured a position for their mothers. Until recently, women in Uganda and in most of Africa could not own property. If a woman did not have a son, she was at the mercy of the clan and her husband's kin if her husband died before her.

My mother had trouble understanding why the boy, my brother, was not named the Hungarian way. The only way she knew. The father's name—simple and to the point, a clear indication of his father's identity. In fact, she was somewhat disturbed that he was not given my father's name. One of her friends, the kind of friend who knows all (we all have at least one of those), told my mother it was so that he could have a way out when they got to Africa. She had done research on this, and this was a worrying trend. But my mother saw pride when my dad dealt with his son; she saw the look of a content man. She could not reconcile this with what her friend was telling her. And anyway, this son did have a compromise. He would have his father's first name, but he would be named according to the rules of the clan. He was very important, and his name would mean something when mentioned in the clan and in the tribe.

PATRICIA TIBBS

The daughter was also named according to the rules of the clan. I was named, as all first born girls were, after my paternal grandmother. I would have a Christian name because my parents were Christians, but this was not what was important. No, that name did not matter much in the big picture. The traditional name carried all the weight. It told a story, a story of family and unbreakable cords, a story of lineage and belonging.

⌘

The nurse had reached the fourth tap on her paper when my husband turned to me with a quizzical look on his face. He looked amused, and later told me he had never quite thought this through. I just was. I just was my father's daughter …and my mother's daughter. And whereas he knew my clan, he had never reached the end of his thoughts when he tried to think in terms of race. But at the time, his look brought my thoughts into sharp focus. Ultimately, I had been raised as my father's child. I am *Ongoda*, and therefore black like my father. I realized then that my hesitation had nothing to do with the fact that I was uncertain of who I was. I always knew who I was. I am merely amused at everyone else's attempts to put me into a category. But no one had ever asked me what I am.

"Black."

The nurse had an odd look as the information was recorded. It occurred to me then that this must not be a common experience for her. Ultimately, it did not matter.

I was sure of who I was.

PATRICIA TIBBS

Gold

Setbacks Are a Part of Life

Definitely gold.

That was my feeling as I laid eyes on my first-born daughter. For most people, the skin color of a child they are about to have is not a concern. The baby will be the same as his father and mother, as it has been for generations before. My cousins in Hungary were most concerned about eye color. "Are his eyes blue?" What is it with blue eyes? I even learned a folk song in Hungarian about blue eyes, which my father promptly changed to suit himself. My cousins in Uganda don't even have that to worry about! All the babies have brown eyes. I had not consciously thought about this because I never consciously thought in those terms. I do when forced to by a question or situation, but then I always slide back to this color-neutral mode that is difficult to explain even to myself. When I looked down at this child that the LORD had blessed me with, I realized that I had subconsciously wondered. My baby's golden beauty reminded me of a time past, the first time of only a few recollections I have of instances when I was forced to think about my skin color.

⌘

I and a friend were running home in the evening. It was still warm enough that we had worked up a sweat. The setting sun's rays were shimmering through the trees we were running under. In these gentle beams, my skin shone gold with the beads of sweat trickling down. We were running because we were scared. It was 1972. President Idi Amin, a dictator who ruled Uganda as a vicious autocrat for eight years from 1971 to 1979, had just announced that all Indians were to be expelled from the country. Apparently he had seen this in a dream. This was one of many dreams he had that would cause so much upheaval and strife in Uganda. We had

PATRICIA TIBBS

been watching the television at another friend's house. Few people had televisions back then. My family had only recently acquired one, but we could only watch it when Dad got home. So it was in this neighbor's home that we had heard the news. Someone in the room had made the comment that I looked like an Indian and I might have to leave too. I was scared. At the time, it appeared to make total sense that I might be forced to leave too if Idi Amin mistook me for an Indian.

As we ran, I could only conjure up horrible thoughts of what would happen to me if we disobeyed Idi Amin. Even at my tender age, I clearly remembered the public executions that had taken place a month or so ago of people who had disobeyed the president. People in my father's tribe were beginning to disappear. I would listen to the adults talking about how Uncle So-and-so had "disappeared." I longed to ask what that meant. Were they in another realm, possibly in the same room, ready to reappear at any time? Had they gone to another country? I knew about other countries because my mother was from another country. A lot of my friends were confused about the concept. At the time, to them, there was Uganda, maybe Kenya and Zaire, perhaps Somalia, and definitely England. The rest was a blur for most of my friends. My mother's country, Hungary, was a stretch of the imagination, and the topic of conversation among us almost always veered toward food when the subject came up.

But worst of all, had Idi Amin killed them and not told anyone?

I longed to ask, but I never did. These conversations were always held in Luo. My mother did not yet understand what was being said, but my dad would translate later. No one knew it at the time, and I did not let on, but I understood Luo much better than I could speak it. Because I did not speak well, no one paid much attention when I was in the room. But I always understood most of what was said.

People were disappearing.

⌘

"Wait!"

My friend halted in midstride.

"You are not golden like the Indians; you are golden in an African way. Or maybe in a European way?" The girl looked a little put out that the argument was not coming together. "Anyway, I do not think Idi Amin meant you. All he has to do is come to your house and he will see."

Idi Amin's coming to my house did not sit well either.

⌘

I burst into the house expecting to find mayhem and confusion. Visions of suitcases open and clothes strewn about with my mother running from room to room packing were brought to a grinding halt. My mother was sitting at the sewing machine with two pins in her mouth, not looking at all like there was an emergency. My one-year-old sister was building a block tower. My brother was trying his best to draw yet another picture of a horse. He was fascinated by them and talked about them constantly. The fact that there were no horses in Uganda did not deter him. This particular rendition of a horse drew a comment from my then three-year-old sister that resulted in yet another fight between them. How could they fight over such nonsense when we could be forced to separate at any time? My father was not yet home. Maybe the news had not gotten here yet. I proceeded to blurt out my concerns to my mother, but I could not quite get my story straight.

"The Indians are leaving, and they told me I might have to leave too if Idi Amin decides I am one of them. So he has to come to our house to see for himself that I am not an Indian, but he can't come to the house because then someone might disappear and—"

She stopped me in mid-sentence. "What are you talking about? Stop talking nonsense, and go clean yourself up. You are all sweaty." Sweat? Who could worry about sweat at a time like this? I decided she might be in denial or something. Anyway, my dad would know what to do.

⌘

The Indians disappeared. I had some good friends who were Indians. I did not know where they went. Almost fifty thousand Indians and other Asians

PATRICIA TIBBS

were forced to leave Uganda at that time. They were forced to leave quickly and could take almost nothing with them. I would like to say that the Ugandans helped them as much as they could to help make it easy, but I think that would be a lie. Most of them left, very bitter, with nothing that they could not put into a suitcase. People said they got what they deserved, but this would be a lie too. Nobody deserves to be driven out of their homes and lives at the whim of another. Everybody has a right to build for themselves a life with the talents they have been given. Over the next three years more people disappeared.

The Europeans disappeared. They had more time. They were able to pack up their households and leave on a planned schedule, for the most part. At least that is the way I remember it. My classes at school that used to look like the United Nations became all Ugandan. Most times I was the only one who was different. This did not concern me too much at the time, and I never consciously felt different. I do not remember noticing the change at the time. It was only later when I looked at class pictures that I registered the fact.

My father's tribesmen were disappearing one by one. Most of them were never seen again. Some managed to escape, but many were captured and their bodies never found. Idi Amin had a particular vendetta against my father's tribe because the former president, Milton Obote, whom he over threw in a military coup in 1971 was from this tribe. He managed to wipe out an entire generation of men. My brief concern that I may have to leave did not concern me again.

⌘

Things got hard. Even then, I noticed the difference. There were food shortages all the time. We lined up for sugar, salt, cornmeal, milk, and bread. There were lines for everything. We had always had cheese, bread, and chocolate in the house. Now there was only what one could harvest from one's farm. But no one in the city had a farm. My father went to his village in the north whenever he could. He would return with sacks of dry foods. This would sustain the family for weeks and sometimes

PATRICIA TIBBS

months. I sometimes wondered as I got older how my mother took this.

My mother now lived very simply, as did all the Ugandans around us. But Ilona adapted. Was there ever any regret about her decision? Did she ever wish she could return to Hungary? Sometimes I would see a sad look on my mother's face, a wistful look of how things could have been. But it was never verbalized. My mother was not one to dwell on what could have been. The hardship was acknowledged and lived through. There was no moping or whining. Those years, she taught us children how to make do. We were never to think that anything was owed us. Anything that we would be blessed with in the future would be worked for and appreciated.

I watched my mother not quit. I think she did suggest to my father that it might be better if we left. But my father was adamant that this was where we all belonged. Once this was decided, she just buckled down and continued in the work of raising her children, working, and caring for the multiple relatives and kinfolk that would show up at the door looking for help. Times were dire, but I do not recall it as a time of sadness. My mother was content and had an inner joy that the circumstances around her could not take away. We went as a family to line up for essentials like salt and sugar. She would put me and later my brother in lines for different things. We also always had cousins living with us. This system allowed us to cut down on the time spent lining up.

⌘

This could have gone on uninterrupted for a few more years, but in the middle of it all, my mother discovered a lump in her breast and was diagnosed with cancer. That was one of the few times I saw my mother cry.

My mother did not cry when the clansmen got together and informed my father, their son and brother that he would have to take a Luo wife because the one he had was not a proper one. My dad was floundering in his decision about this because he did not like to break tradition. He was a doctor and better educated than all the clansmen around him, but he did not want to disrespect them. He instilled this respect in his children. Ultimately, my grandmother, his mother, Tata to me, broke all protocol and chased all the clansmen off because their son already had an heir, an heir who had already been named according to the clan naming rules.

A woman standing up to men was not heard of very often. But my grandmother was past caring. Tata had realized early on that her son would do whatever he set his mind to. The fact that he had not married a second wife, a Ugandan, by then meant that he was not inclined to. She was tired of all those men gathering around her table and making her unique daughter-in-law angry. Tata had already made a name for herself by leaving her harsh and abusive husband, who had several other wives. Her older brother, who was a chief with several wives of his own and who was wealthy at that time by village standards, took her and her four children in. That is the only way she had survived. My dad's determination and will came from her. He was determined to get to a place that would ensure his mother was well taken care of. He remembered his father taunting his mother that she would be back because she had nothing. Indeed she had nothing. She could own nothing. But she had a brother.

My dad had a long memory. I never met my paternal grandfather; my great uncle on the other hand, he was very important to my father, and he made sure we knew him well.

My mother did not even cry when Mama came to visit us in Uganda from Hungary. This was a very emotional and exciting time.

⌘

The grandmothers were so similar, and yet so different.

Both were of medium height and lean. Both were used to hard work and had raised four children farming the land. For both, the child in this marriage was the smartest of the four and was the only one who had a university education. Both had graying hair.

But, one had blue eyes, the other dark brown. One used to be blonde, the other jet black. One was deeply tanned, the other deeply ebonized. One was the patient wife of a sometimes-drunk-but-hard-working man. The other was the estranged wife of a man who had several other wives.

PATRICIA TIBBS

⌘

My mother did not cry when she saw me act as interpreter for my grandmothers. I was the only one apart from my dad who could speak both languages. I sat between the two and interpreted between them in simple Luo and fluent Hungarian. There was a short period in my life when I was fluent in both languages, but at the time, I was still mastering Luo. I was also trying to master English. I sometimes wondered about the human brain. I was mastering two completely different languages and fluent in a third, and I rarely mixed them up. My younger sisters and brothers always mixed up the two languages. This made for interesting sentences that began in one language and ended in another, causing much hilarity in the home. I suppose this was because I was the only one who was old enough to have both languages spoken as the primary language around me. When we were in Hungary, everyone spoke Hungarian. When we got to Uganda, my parents spoke Hungarian to each other, but everyone else spoke Luo, and later English. My brother had been too young when we left Hungary.

✽

My mother did not cry when one clansman then another would disappear. She worried about Dad's safety, but he was so deeply patriotic that he would not leave unless he was forced to. My dad was a quiet man. This kept him off of Idi Amin's list for many years. I am not sure if Idi Amin had a list, but in my mind he did. In my mind, he had a list that he checked off when he killed someone. Some of the killings were very public; some were private, only witnessed by the family; and some were secret. Those were the ones no one knew about until an absence could not be explained. Whenever my dad was late coming home, there was nothing to do but worry. There was no telephone in the home, and cell phones were still a quarter of a century away.

✽

But my mother did cry when cancer was found. After much discussion and tears, my dad decided that it would be best if she went back to Hungary for treatment. Cancer treatment in Uganda was very rudi-

PATRICIA TIBBS

mentary at the time, and my dad had connections with doctors in Szeged with whom he had trained. Mama was both sad and glad when Ilona arrived home for treatment. Dunafoldvar had changed, and the differences between my mother's life now and what it could have been would have swayed a lesser woman. A mastectomy and radiotherapy were done. While she recovered, and between treatments, she stayed at home with her parents. The people in the village gossiped.

"He has finally tired of her. Look. She is back without the children, and she has been crying a lot."

Mama was concerned about all the weepiness. This was not like the child that they knew. She completely misunderstood the reason for it.

"Was he bad to you? You do not have to go back. There is some land behind Pista's (my uncle) that you could farm and build a house on. You could teach at the secondary school. You will be happy again."

My mother stopped crying. She was not one to talk much, but she was frustrated that she could not weep for what she had lost without giving everyone the wrong impression.

"I am still alive, and this …this life, this place is no longer me."

She thought about chocolate and bread, apples and juice, ice cream and bacon, new clothes and shoes. She surely did miss having them. Then she thought about another woman raising her children…. not for all the chocolate in the world.

"He is a good man. My children …What will happen to them without me? He will marry another woman …a 'proper one,' who will mistreat my children. As long as God gives me life, I will stay with him. If I do not, what will happen to my children? I must do whatever is within my power to ensure that my children fulfill their God-given destiny. If I leave him now, they will not be the same. The opportunities that they may have because I am there will not be there anymore. The cord will be broken, and there is no blessing in that. If I am only thinking of myself, then I would have no reason to go back. There are killings every day. There are shortages of everything. I cannot even make bread! His brothers do not like me, jealousy abounds, and some of the meanness that I experience could cripple me. I do not yet speak the language, so sometimes they

PATRICIA TIBBS

talk about me in my presence, but I am learning! Yes, I want better things for myself. Yes, I could do without all the drama. Yes, you were right. It is so hard. But he will be a great man one day. And when he is, my children will be right there in the umbrella of his greatness. He is not a perfect man, and I have wondered often about the rightness of my decision. But he needs a trusted woman by his side. One who will not betray his efforts and malign him. He needs a good mother for his children, and I am it."

Mama was silent for a long time after my mother angrily vented her frustration at being misunderstood. But a new understanding came to her that day. She realized for the first time how mistaken she had been. Until then, she had regarded these grandchildren of hers as a liability, a problem to be worried about and dealt with. That day she realized that just maybe God had taken her daughter to Uganda for a very special purpose. She realized how unique her son-in-law was. He was still married to her daughter and had not taken on an African wife as all the other Africans eventually did when they returned home. Her daughter and son-in-law were raising children with a strong foundation. Mama realized that she had done well after all. She had raised a strong Magyar woman who would have a lasting impact on a small African country. No one else in the village would have that kind of impact on the world. Not then anyway.

"Okay, Ilonka, I get it. You go back to your husband. I am so proud of you!"

⌘

My mother returned to Uganda in the midst of more killings. Would they ever stop? At the airport, my dad, the other three children and I were there to meet our mother, and his wife. It was a hot day, and we were all sweating, our skin shone gold in the midday sun. A huddle of white, gold, and black shimmered briefly, a multicolored cord still strong and yet unbreakable because each braid that went into it had been well prepared.

⌘

My thoughts were interrupted when the baby cried out. I looked down at her tenderly. The child was beautiful, my first born. I unhooked my bra, and my

PATRICIA TIBBS

infant girl noisily latched on and began to suckle. A golden head on a light brown breast with a black hand gently stroking the baby's cheeks. I looked up at my husband and smiled.

Another cord was being braided.

White

Know Your Heritage

That is exactly what he was. As with each of the other children, I realized that I had subconsciously wondered what he would look like. I did not need an ultrasound scan to tell me that this time I carried a boy. I just knew.

He looked white. I was surprised. But even as I registered this, it passed quickly because I never dwell on skin color for long. As always, when I am faced with a situation where I have to consciously acknowledge the color of someone's skin, the thought never lasts longer than it takes to register the fact. I wonder about this sometimes when I have time to dwell on it or when I am faced with someone who appears to make decisions based on the skin color of the person they are dealing with or talking to. I wonder if they do this subconsciously or if it is a habit born of long programming by the environment in which they were raised.

Was I also somehow "programmed" by the circumstances into which I was born? If that is so, then racial tensions should eventually become nonexistent. When I was a child, I knew of only two other families like ours. Now it is so common. Do all these children think the same way I do? Do they have this color-neutral zone in which they operate? The amazing thing is that I have never had to verbalize this at all. It was never necessary, and it is not something you bring up in everyday conversation. It's not that I do not notice the color of everyone's skin; if I am asked, I usually know, but it has amazed me that I sometimes cannot recall. I would not make a good police witness. But unless I am asked, it hardly ever surfaces to the conscious level.

As I looked at my newborn son, I mused about my childhood. What is it about having babies that makes you think deep thoughts? One moment in time came to me in a rush. It was 1974.

 PATRICIA TIBBS

"Yes, you white, come here!"

I turned to look at who might be calling me. Three children: one boy, who was obviously practicing his English, and two girls. The boy was probably a little younger than I was; the girls were little more than toddlers. The youngest girl, who looked to be close to three years old, was dressed only in an old skirt that was once blue but was now an indeterminate shade of brown with a blue hue. She was barefoot, as were all the children in the village during that time. Chubby cheeks with beautiful black skin and a look of health were evidence that her mother was still breastfeeding her. Round, dark-brown eyes looked up at me as if I was something she had not seen before. The second girl was older and had taken on the slightly malnourished look that was typical of children in this semi-arid area in northern Uganda. This four- or five-year-old had long, skinny legs, a protuberant abdomen, sparse brown hair that was a harsh contrast to dark skin, and ribs that were very easy to count. She was also dressed in a torn skirt of indeterminate color, but the happy expression on her face made me smile. I looked from the girls to the boy. He looked triumphant.

"This is what a white person looks like," he explained in Luo. As usual, he was sure I did not understand what he was saying. That could not be possible.

"Does she eat people?" the older girl asked in Luo.

"Yes. If you misbehave, she will come and get you in the night." This brought fear into the eyes of the girls. The smiles disappeared. He then switched to heavily accented English. "I was just telling them that if they are good, you will give us some sweets."

How quaint. I was not amused. I turned to them fully and told them all in fluent Luo that I only ate liars so their brother was in trouble. They fled.

I turned back and continued on my way. I was walking to my grandmother Tata's compound to join my cousins who were already busy threshing millet. The crop had been big that year. This was good. The millet harvested at this time would sustain families for the whole year until the next crop. It had rained just enough, and food was abundant. This was not always the case. Some years, there was

PATRICIA TIBBS

semi-starvation by the time the crop was ready for harvest. Millet formed the foundation of the diet of the Luo peoples of Northern Uganda. It was present at every meal we ate at Tata's home. I did not realize then that it is one of those things that is difficult to eat day in and day out. It just was the food one ate there.

⌘

The compound consisted of a cleared circular area approximately forty feet across with compacted earth that was as firm as any wooden or concrete floor. When it rained, the water would run off this area and dry quickly. It rarely ever got muddy. Around this area were five structures. The largest one was a semi-permanent square building made of mud bricks with a layer of cement over it. A tin roof, two wooden doors on opposite ends of the building, and wooden window shutters completed the outside of the main house. There was a veranda across the entire front of the house with wooden poles supporting the roof. Gutters ran along the entire edge of the roof with a spout that directed all rainwa-

CORDS

ter coming off the roof into a large tank that sat to the right side of the veranda. Harvesting rainwater was very important because there was no plumbing indoors or outside.

Inside were four rooms. A small hallway from the front had doors to three of the rooms; the fourth room came off one of the other three in the back. The largest room was not much more than ten feet across. This often housed the cotton harvest until it was baled and sold. Sometimes on rainy days, it was used for the evening gatherings that always happened after supper.

The other three rooms were not much larger than six feet across. Tata's bedroom was in front and to the left. It was always dark in there. The window was rarely opened and the only lighting available was from two kerosene lamps used in the entire compound. More lamps were only needed when my father was in residence. Although he was building a modern three-bedroom house nearby, he spent every waking minute in Tata's compound unless he was traveling in the villages checking on people or touring the fields. One lamp went everywhere with my grandmother after dark, the second being used

PATRICIA TIBBS

by whoever was living there at the time. This varied over the years, but there were always two or more people. Often they were grandchildren or nieces and nephews. They lived in the home and helped with the chores.

My father always made sure his mother was well cared for. He visited often and took his wife and children back home regularly. That is why I was there. My father made sure his children learned the way of his people. I would be returning to Kampala at the end of the week by bus. An aunt would accompany me.

⌘

I came to my grandmother and knelt down. That is the way a girl child greets her elders. Women used to greet men that way too. This has changed some. A woman in general kneeling to greet men in general is a dying custom now. I greeted her with the morning greeting and was offered tea. There was some leftover roasted cassava to have with the tea. I ate quickly, impatient to join in the work. My grandmother sent me into the main house to collect

CORDS

a threshing stick. It was eight in the morning, but the rooms were dark as usual. I stood for a minute in the dark and began to notice the shapes around me. There were several large water pots sitting on dry banana fiber bases in the shape of a doughnut. The doughnut shape gave the huge earthenware pots a firm base. There was an old cabinet that had once had doors. In the corner were several pipes used for drinking local beer. I did not see a threshing stick. On my way out, I peeped into my grandmother's bedroom. There was a twin bed made of wood with a good, firm mattress and clean bedding. Several items of clothing hung from a rope that was attached to nails on opposite ends of the room. There was a cabinet and a small table both piled with books, kitchen items, and other random articles that were considered too important to be anywhere else. This was not a typical village bedroom. Few people had a bed or bedding. Many only had one set of clothes that was washed intermittently. Until the clothes were dry, many went around only minimally clad, often with an old piece of cloth. I suppose that this could be disconcerting to a visitor, but I was used

PATRICIA TIBBS

to women walking around with bare chests, their breasts dancing around as they walked.

This had disconcerted my mother at first. It was strange. I do not think that my mother ever quite got used to it. Tata must have realized this and never did walk around with breasts bare as most of the village women did. I wondered if it was also due to the fact that it was not necessary. Tata had adequate clothing. Her son, my father, made sure of that. There are advantages to having a doctor for a son.

⌘

I came out of the main house squinting in the bright sunlight. I called out to Tata, telling her the stick was not there.

"Check in the kitchen."

I walked across the compound toward the kitchen. This was a grass-thatched hut with mud walls. The thatch on the roof was neat and well maintained. My dad made sure of that. The walls were sturdy and smooth. I walked into the hut and was immediately assailed by the thick smoke that characterized the inside of the kitchen. It was a matter of pride that I not cough or sneeze. True Luo people did not do that. I bent down to get out of the worst of the smoke and looked around.

To the left of the door, an earthenware pot sat on three large, roughly round stones. The stones formed a tripod base on which the pot fitted well. A log and several twigs stretched out from between the stones under the pot, forming a haphazard star. I noticed that the beans in the pot had stopped boiling. The fire needed to be adjusted. I expertly shook the log and twigs, pushing them into the middle of the tripod under the pot. I took a deep breath and blew carefully, controlling my breath as my grandmother had taught me. The embers glowed red for several seconds followed soon by several tongues of fire that leapt up toward the pot. A bubbling sound from the pot a minute later indicated that the fire was adequate.

I looked around at the walls and about the floor. My aunt had recently polished the walls and the floor with a concoction of cow dung and mud. It sounded distasteful, but it did make the walls look good. I spotted the object of my search, which was

PATRICIA TIBBS

nothing more than a sturdy stick, about four feet long and half an inch wide. It had been polished with oil from a Yao tree. I grabbed it and ran out, taking up a place in the circle of women and girls who were threshing.

The millet had recently been harvested and was now dry. The seeds, still attached to the fingers and stems, were put into a heap and beaten repetitively to separate the seeds and the chaff. This process was not random. There was a rhythm to it. All the women knelt down. Holding the stick at one end with both hands, it was brought around to the left of one's body in a circular motion and then up over one's head, bringing it down with maximum force. The circular motion ensured that maximum force was applied with minimum effort. This would not be possible with a simple up and down motion.

For a while, nothing would be heard but the rhythmic thudding as sticks went up, around, and down. During a pause in the threshing, I looked up to see a small crowd that had gathered on the path close by. A white person in the village threshing grain was an aberration. It was 1974. The only white person known to many of them was the Catholic priest. After a while, they moved on. Many had heard about my family by now but were still surprised when they saw one of us acting as if we had been born there.

Tata sent me to the granary to fetch the sorting baskets. The granary was located at the edge of the compound across from the kitchen. At that time, there was only one; later there would be three as the family grew. The granary was shaped like a pumpkin with the top quarter cut off and replaced with a thatch roof. It was round at the bottom and elevated about two to three feet off the ground held by thick logs. The walls were made of interwoven reeds that were then covered with a thick layer of muddy clay much like the walls of the kitchen were. In here, the grain was stored, dry and safe from the animals. I climbed up the log frame and reached inside the granary for the five sorting baskets. These were about two feet, square-shaped, woven baskets with a concave surface giving them the appearance of a large, square, shallow bowl. They were made of tightly interwoven reeds that were then smeared with a thick layer of the muddy cow dung concoc-

PATRICIA TIBBS

tion. Once dry, these were very useful in the millet preparing process.

Calabash-fulls (gourds) of the millet with the chaff were placed onto the baskets. In a designated area, the women held the basket over their heads and slowly poured the contents down over one shoulder standing in such a way that the wind would blow most of the chaff away, leaving the millet to drop close to their feet. This activity would stop whenever the wind died down and resume quickly when wind was detected.

Next, the semi-sorted millet was again loaded onto the sorting baskets. These were then grasped firmly with both hands at one end, and then with a slight upward motion, the contents of the front end of the basket were made to fly up into the air in a very precise motion that resulted in all the millet landing back on the basket. Blowing at the millet, again in that controlled way Luo children learned early in life, resulted in more of the chaff falling in front of the basket while the millet grains landed back into the basket. A very complex rhythmic shaking of the baskets resulted in what was left of the chaff separating from the grain in a very precise fashion. The grain was then inspected, and any left-over chaff was physically removed. Sacks were then filled, ready to be ground or for storage.

⌘

This process lasted the whole day and was tiring. It had taken much practice to figure out how to throw the millet up in the air and not lose all of it at my feet. The rhythmic shaking motion was tricky and fascinating to watch. I never quite got the hang of it, probably because I did not practice enough. After the work was done, the compound was swept and the chaff thrown out into the fields.

⌘

As the sun began to set, my grandmother sent me out to the surrounding bush to bring in the goats. I went with my cousins. I found two goats, both females, nursing a kid each. The kids were not tied up until they were older. They spent the day romping between their mother and the compound. I was always fascinated at the fact that each kid new its mother's bleat and would answer when called! At

PATRICIA TIBBS

this time of the day, they were loud and impatient to come back in. I brought the goats into the compound, or, more precisely, they brought me back, dragging me and straining on their ropes. I allowed them to go to the salt lick and to drink some water, and then I tied them to a post in the goat shed. This structure consisted of several rough wooden poles in a ring around a central pole with a thatch roof over it. My cousin always came and checked my knots and almost invariably moved one of the goats to another pole. Oops! Wrong pole! Apparently the goats were disturbed if they were not in their usual place.

⌘

The chickens would begin to enter the kitchen at sunset after a full day of free range scratching and pecking. Each chicken knew where it belonged. Through the day, I would see many chickens in the yard, but at the end of the day, those that did not belong to Tata went back home to roost in their own homes. My grandmother knew each one of her twenty-odd chickens by sight. If one did not show up, she sent someone to look for it. Intermittently, one was eaten or given as a gift or new ones bought or received as gifts; she still knew them all! Not one of them looked like the other to a trained eye. Tata had tried to train me in the fine art of differentiating chickens, but that was a lost cause. I could tell a rooster from a hen. That was the extent of my expertise.

One day she had sent me and my cousins to look for a rooster that had not returned. I tried to chase every rooster we met back to Tata's home, and they would not go! My cousins had a good laugh about this. They watched me run circles around several roosters, even giving me tips on the best way to go about chasing them home. This would go on for several minutes until they could stand it no more and burst out laughing telling me, "That is not the one." Amazingly, we did find this errant rooster who it turned out was "flirting with the girls." He was very easy to herd home once he was "reminded" that it was time to go. All we had to do was get between him and some busy looking hens. He gave us a look of disdain and went marching straight back to my grandmother's kitchen several hundred yards away,

PATRICIA TIBBS

only stopping to peck at a random plant or ant just to let us know he was still in charge. When I thought we should hurry him because he was wasting time, I was told that he would only run in the opposite direction we needed to go just to teach us a lesson. I thought this was a joke but I did not feel inclined to test the theory. I knew for a fact that I for one would not be able to identify him again, and I was often tired by that time.

⌘

A meal of beans flavored with peanut butter and millet bread was served. I was still polishing the fine art of making millet bread, which involved nothing more than boiling water and stirring in millet flour to form thick, brown dough. It sounds simple enough, but if not made well, it is lumpy, too runny, or burnt. It was dough that if not stirred and mixed just right would cause burns to the skin as it bubbled up in miniature explosions, stick to the pan, or cause the whole pan to go flying off the stove. I was intimately experienced with all three disasters. But I learned.

⌘

The men sat at the small table, while the women and children sat on goat hides or mats on the floor. One bowl of millet and one of beans was shared by all. The men had theirs, and the women had theirs. Individual plates were not used at the time. Silverware was never used. The rules were precise. Hand washing was meticulous.

You nabbed a piece of millet bread the size of a mouthful with your fingers, molding it into a ball in the same hand. You never used both hands, and you never switched hands. You then expertly poked a hole on one side of it, creating a miniature pot. Then you filled this "pot" with the sauce, dipping once. You never licked your fingers while at table. This way of eating gradually disappeared as time passed. But at that time, it was the only way we ate at Tata's house.

⌘

I had a bath in the bath house with cold water in a basin. I would fetch this water from the water

PATRICIA TIBBS

pump a mile away. At that age, I could easily carry a twenty-liter can (five gallons) of water on my head, a feat I was later unable to accomplish. When I tried many years later, after medical school, I thought the spinal spasm would result in some sort of paralysis. I had swung the water can up onto my head in an expert fashion with no problem. Even I admired me! I took a couple of steps. The pain was excruciating. I brought the can down in a hurry and was quite convinced that my top two vertebrae had sunk into the third one. My body had lost that adaptation. It had been necessary to carry water like this at one time, but not anymore. Now I could pay someone to fetch it for me. Someone got a temporary job that day.

⌘

Later that week, it was time for me to return to Kampala, where my parents lived. I had to get to the town twenty miles away to catch the Kampala-bound bus. This was achieved first by bicycle and then riding on the back of a 'pickup' truck that was overflowing with people, chickens, a goat, and a bicycle. I have ridden on these flatbed trucks often.

It never ceases to amaze me how they never really get full. I was squished between bodies and luggage with something feathery at my feet, which I discovered to be a chicken when it tried to investigate the edibility of my toenail. Every few hundred feet we would stop to take on or let off some passengers. I had been warned that if I complained, they would let me off. I did not complain. I just found something I could hang on to—the corner of a heavy sack—and clung to it for dear life.

My aunt and I boarded the bus headed for Kampala. We had a seat. Most of the passengers did not. The bus that was made for forty-eight people had what looked like one hundred people in it. Most stood or sat in the aisle. There were chickens under the seats; a young goat was in the aisle squashed in with people and luggage. I looked at my aunt, I was a little worried. I had never ridden in a bus before, but the books I read had pictures of buses in England, and they did not look like this. Well, the crowding anyway. I had seen a dog in a bus in one of my stories, and I decided at the time that this was probably no different from having a chicken or a goat. My aunt did not seem perturbed

PATRICIA TIBBS

by this. She was busy adjusting the straps and layers of her *Gomesi*. This traditional dress is beautiful but consists of many layers of loose clothing, which can only be controlled by an expert. A naïve woman could quickly lose the various ends of the ensemble and find herself exposed!

So with a honk from the horn, a loud bleat from the goat, and a lot of clucking from various chickens, we were off. The sounds of laughter and conversation gradually faded as the hours went by. I got a lot of glances my way, usually with bits of conversation about the presence of the white child on the bus. This conversation washed over me; I was used to it. Eventually the even droning of the bus lulled me to sleep.

⌘

I stared at my son as I came back to the present, white like my mother. Even as the thought registered in my mind, I had moved on to other things, like how much he looked like my brother. I looked up at my husband; he was smiling as he named him.

He was important. He was the heir and was named according to the rules of the clan. I knew that my husband had not worried about having a fourth girl; the days when a son was of utmost importance were fading. But now there was a son, and that changed something. He was of the *Muhesi* clan.

I would always be *Ongoda*. I would always be his mother. The men and women of the *Ongoda* clan would be born to my brothers.

New braids were being added.

And the cords thicken as new braids are added. As the clans intertwine they become one cord. One could choose to pull a braid out of the cord, it would not be difficult because each braid is distinct, but it would weaken the cord.

PATRICIA TIBBS

Negro

Find Your Niche

This word brought me abruptly out of my musings. I was rolling some thoughts around in my head when I was roused to awareness because of this word. It had been a long time since I had heard it. I am always fascinated by the workings of the human mind. During anatomy lab, dissection of the brain had been somewhat depressing. It was difficult to fathom that this mass of gray-looking tissue had once been the seat of great thoughts. My mind had moved at amazing speed from thoughts about my children, a pressing engagement the next week, and I was in the middle of trying to work through a knotty situation at work when I tuned back in to my surroundings.

I was at a reception at an acquaintance's home in a small town in the Deep South. My family had been living in a town close by for a little over ten years. Mississippi had been an ideal place for us. The pace was much slower than in the Midwest, traffic was minimal, and strong bonds of friendship had been formed. The children were thriving, our church family was wonderful, and my husband was content. I enjoyed my work immensely. In this slow-paced town, I was able to balance work and home life. I thanked God for this. I was confident that my father and mother had prepared me well for any tasks that might come my way, but this opportunity to work in a small town had been such a blessing.

There had been loud conversation around me. I had not joined in because it was a topic that held only minimal interest to me. Hunting was a regular topic among my mostly male peers. I often listened with casual interest, sometimes wondering if my son would ever learn to hunt.

Unfortunately, guns always brought on negative emotions. I had needed to figure out why this was

PATRICIA TIBBS

so because it was the basis of much male bonding in Mississippi. Many of the stories I heard during these times were recounted with much gusto and a lot of pride. Very positive. Sons were reared in the tradition, and much training of young men occurred while handling a gun.

It was not difficult for me to figure this one out. For me, guns had always been associated with the killing of people. The common folk had no access to guns to protect themselves and therefore were at the mercy of those in political power who did. I still have flashbacks in my unguarded moments of running from soldiers, completely at their mercy and powerless to defend myself. Hunting in my father's village had been done with spears, traps, and machetes. No one owned a gun. It was going to take at least another generation for that perception to change. There have been a few times in my life when my family and I have been cowering in the house at the complete mercy of someone trying to invade our home with a gun. Many friends I grew up with have had similar experiences, and for many of them, family members were killed during these attacks.

It is at those times when I wished my dad and my friend's dads had owned a gun. I have always wondered how many dads, moms, and children would still be alive if families were able to defend themselves during such attacks. On the other hand, I also knew of family feuds that could have ended terribly if someone had owned a gun. I recall one particular incident where two men, members of my father's clan, began one evening in a cordial fashion. Both got somewhat inebriated and began an argument that ended in a fight. One of them went into the house and returned with a machete. I always shudder when I think that this could have been a gun.

⌘

I wondered when in the conversation the topic had moved on from the latest unfortunate deer. I realized I must have tuned out for a while.

"Over my dead body will a Negro be the president of the United States of America."

I was shocked at the emotion but also somewhat amused. I hoped the gentleman was planning

PATRICIA TIBBS

his eulogy because it looked somewhat inevitable. I could not prevent the smile on my face. People do say the most ridiculous things. Intelligence does not appear to protect one from uttering nonsense once in a while. I am just as guilty as the next person. I had not heard that word or the word *nigger* for a long time. In fact, the few times I had heard it uttered recently had always been when one African American was mad at another as in, "If that nigger don't get my tires did, there will be hell to pay!" I thought back to my family's visit to Mama in Hungary when I was twelve.

⌘

"Hey, Negro!"

I turned toward the call, wondering to whom they were referring. It was 1977. I was riding a bicycle through the downtown area of Dunafoldvar with my grandmother and my cousin ahead of me. The downtown area of Dunafoldvar was picturesque and quaint. Some of the buildings were really old. There is a church there that I hear was built in seventeen something, St. Anne's church. I loved to go into the building and look around. It was magnificent, and still is I think. There is amazing artwork that I was told is in the Baroque style, with carvings and statues of angels and various saints. That was my favorite building, and we were headed there even though it was not Sunday. I had to turn back to prevent myself from crashing into the next pole.

"Yes, you!"

That was new. I had been living here for a month now and had never heard myself called in that fashion. People did refer to me as a Negro, but it had only been in descriptive terms like one would use to describe the person they were talking about. I had grown to accept this. But this degrading sound to the word was new.

I stopped to look at the person calling to me. He was a boy not much older than me. I was amused to note that he did not look very Hungarian himself. He had brown hair and skin that looked darker than mine! Now that was amazing. I was about to yell back to this boy about how he was more of a Negro than I was. I wondered why I had the instinct to do this because I did not at the time associate the word with any negative thoughts. It was just a descrip-

PATRICIA TIBBS

tive term to me. But he had called me a name. It could have been "chicken" or "Catholic" or "bread pudding" with the same results. It was the way he had used the word that had bothered me, and the fact that he looked just like me!

My grandmother stopped me.

"Leave him alone. He is a Gypsy. They are all thieves and troublemakers. He is going nowhere."

Going nowhere? That was not possible; everyone was going somewhere. Everyone had a destiny prepared by God. But I believed my grandmother at the time. I thought then that my dad must have been mistaken on that count. Maybe he had never met a Gypsy? It was many years before I realized that this minute encounter had colored my opinion of the Romani peoples. Was this how it all started for everyone? A seemingly unimportant remark made at the spur of the moment, unthinkingly, by an adult in authority over a child?

When I met a Romani doctor at a convention years later, I realized that I had subconsciously wondered if my father had been wrong. But he had not been wrong. Everyone has a destiny prepared for them by God. One takes the cords handed to one and weaves them diligently into a tapestry worthy of one's gifts.

Parents are to hand their children the best and most precious cords they possess, and children are to receive those cords and begin weaving. Things could go wrong at either end. When parents fail to hand their children the best they have and selfishly weave their own tapestries, neither tapestry is ever as good as it could have been. When children are handed the best from their parents yet fail to weave as they are being taught or lose the cords or worse, decide that they will look for their own, the tapestry is ugly indeed.

⌘

I obeyed my grandmother and let it go. I really did not want to trouble my mother anymore than she already was. My mom and the children had come to Hungary to live with Mama because Idi Amin had finally caught up with my father.

One day my four siblings and I, along with a couple of cousins who were living with us at the time, were playing outside in the yard at home in

PATRICIA TIBBS

Kampala when a large truck of soldiers parked in front of the house. We lived in a comfortable four-bedroom, modern house with running water and electricity and even "servant" quarters. This was in stark contrast to Tata's home in the village in the north, but such a home was common to most of the working-class people in Kampala at the time. The main house and "servant" quarters were designed after typical English homes built in Uganda originally for the British but now taken over by Ugandans since independence in 1962. This style of building has persisted and is predominant in current Ugandan architecture.

We fled into the bushes in the backyard. For over one hour, the soldiers stayed. They were loud and were speaking mostly in Swahili and some rudimentary English. They appeared to be arguing about something. I could not understand what they were saying. I prayed. I prayed a fervent prayer for protection, one of many I prayed in my life while running or hiding from soldiers. All this was happening the day after my parents discovered that their bedroom had been broken into and ransacked, but nothing appeared to have been taken. The soldiers left after a while. They appeared to have come to some sort of decision. My father did not return that day. I did not see him again for almost six months.

⌘

My mother appeared to be very worried. She did not talk much about what happened to my father at the time, so I was left to my own imaginings of what could have happened. When I thought about it, I realized that though I knew that something terrible had happened to my father, I did not think he was dead because of the kind of worrying that my mother exhibited. The worry that a person exhibits when they are unsure if a person they love is alive or dead is different from the worry one exhibits when there is a major change in one's life that reminds one that life is, in essence, uncertain. It is not easy to put into words. But she was worrying about us, about how to contribute to the budget and expenses at Mama's home, and generally acting like this state of affairs was temporary and would end soon. We did not unpack suitcases; we did not enroll in school. So even though it was not verbalized, I realized that we

PATRICIA TIBBS

would be moving on to meet my dad at some point in the future, but it was not clear when.

I later found out that my father had escaped narrowly while he was at work. A few more minutes and the soldiers would have found him. He hid at a close friend's house and travelled to the Kenya border by bus, posing as the deaf and mute nephew of his friend. There were twenty-one heavily armed military road blocks encountered on the way, and at each of them, the whole bus was emptied out, the soldiers looking for fugitives like my dad. It had taken an entire day to travel approximately two hundred miles.

Before he left, he was able to communicate with my mother instructions to sell what could be sold and take the children to Hungary until he was able to communicate his next move. We were out of Uganda within a month.

⌘

Mama had been glad to see us. She had never seen the baby who was then three years old. He was conceived after my mother had been diagnosed with cancer and had received partial treatment. A second course of radiotherapy had been planned for three months after the initial mastectomy and treatment. My mother was given strong advice to have an abortion and return for therapy. My parents ignored this advice and no further therapy was obtained. At my brother's wedding thirty years later, my mother broke down and cried. That was another of the few times I saw her cry. "I just prayed that God would let me live long enough for the child to know me. And look how much more blessing he gave. Praise God! Praise God!"

⌘

Because my mother had been there, six beautiful tapestries had been woven from the cords that were handed down. They may have been good even if she had not been there, but they would have been different.

⌘

Many in the village were skeptical. "The Negro finally tired of her. This time it is for real. Look.

PATRICIA TIBBS

She has brought all the children!" Well, that did not stick this time either, but it did bring some excitement into the otherwise quiet and event-deprived village.

⌘

I became fluent in Hungarian again. Mama taught me how to cook some Magyar dishes; goulash was my favorite. New friends were made. Cousins lived next door and were ready playmates. We did not attend school and generally had a grand time. Mama still lived in the same house that my mother had been raised in. There had been several modernizations to the house. My grandfather had died a few months before, and this caused great sadness in my mother. At the time that he was sick and ailing, my parents were in the middle of the realization that my dad's life was in danger, and my mother had not been able to leave Uganda to come and see her dying father.

⌘

The house had only two bedrooms with a tiny front room between them. A bathroom completed the design of the house. The front bedroom faced the street and was part of the front wall. I spent hours looking out of this window into the street. Cars were few; most of the traffic at the time was horse-drawn buggies. I loved to hear the *clippety-clop* of the horses as they went down the street. The furniture in the room was beautiful wood furniture with intricate carvings. There was a double bed, an armoire, a chair, and a dresser. Several hand-sewn embroidery pieces graced the furniture. My mother had taught me how to hand embroider, and I had made several pieces myself, but these made by my grandmother were exquisite. Mama watched proudly as the grandchildren that once were a cause of worry and pain made beautiful embroidery pieces. The grandchildren she had thought would not fit in. She had a unique family. No one, not one of the women in the village, could claim any such fame.

PATRICIA TIBBS

⌘

The front room had a cupboard where fine china was stored, a beautiful table next to the window, and to one side was the larder. Several sides of ham, lengths of pepperoni, and bacon hung from the ceiling in this room. Dried peppers, shelves of canned food, and some old photographs were to be found on the walls. This was one of my favorite rooms.

The other bedroom had two large beds, one was Mama's, and the other that had belonged to my grandfather I now shared with my sister. There was a small television, a table, and a dresser. Again, the beautiful embroidery abounded. Next to this was a bathroom that had been modernized since my mother had lived there. The bathroom also led out to the stables and then out to the backyard. Mama did not own any more horses, preferring to go everywhere by bicycle or by bus. The stables now contained old bits of equipment and horse paraphernalia. The backyard was full of chickens and some ducks. Four noisy pigs in a pen behind the house provided some entertainment.

✿

When I first saw the chickens, they immediately caught my attention. This was one of the things my grandmothers had in common in their homes: chickens. But there was a big difference. Tata in Uganda knew all the chickens in her possession by sight. Each one was uniquely identifiable because of the multitude of colors. From black to fiery red to brown, green, speckled, striped, and layered. When one was missing, it was looked for on that day and could be identified on sight! Here in Dunafoldvar, all the chickens were brown and white. Mama would only know one was missing if they were counted. One day when this happened, I asked her which one was missing. She gave me a strange look and said, "One of them."

The well was still in the front yard and still in use because the kitchen did not yet have running water. Only the bathroom did. The kitchen, still separated from the main house, was the center of much activity. There we cooked and ate.

Mama owned several vineyards. We would work on the vines, or act like we were working, but this was a favorite place to play "hide and seek." We spent long hours romping around in the sandy soil of the vineyards. There was always homemade wine in the cellar, and wine graced every meal. I am sure the department of child services would have frowned on my grandmother's policy of giving everyone wine. Except the baby. I mean, who in their right mind would give a three-year-old wine? But a twelve-year-old, well, they needed to be taught the right way to drink wine. I do not remember finding it strange. It was just the thing to do. Apart from my grandfather, and one second cousin who had been 'damaged by the war,' not one of them drank to excess. My father continued that tradition. I do not think it hurt my brothers, or my cousins who were directly under his influence. I am sure some-one, somewhere has studied this, but I suspect it is one of those things like obesity, no one really knows why, except that if you eat too much you get fat, and if you drink too much you get drunk.

⌘

Wine, oh yes, that brought me back to the wine I was savoring at the moment. It was definitely not Mama's wine but it was okay. I looked at my wine glass and wondered what to do about the disturbing turn of the conversation around me. I realized that I would do nothing more than listen in as I always do. I have learned that my silence in these situations often speaks much louder than any words I could have used. The gentleman appeared to realize that the landscape in which he now worked was strikingly different than it was when he had first become a doctor. He looked around and seemed very uncomfortable. Eventually he looked up, chancing a look at me. I smiled. He stared at me for several seconds, his discomfort gradually giving way to a look of resignation. He smiled back. The promise of a friendship hung in the air.

Brown

Make a Difference

"Definitely brown! You and I are definitely brown, Mama. That is what I told that boy."

"You mean your friend?" I asked my six-year-old son, who was downing a snack, watching the television, and building some kind of spaceship with his Lego collection all at the same time.

"No, he is not my friend. My friends don't say things like that."

"What things?"

"Like he said I am black or something."

My heart cracked a little. "What did you tell him?"

"I told him I am brown. And he looks brown too, except his hair is white and straight. Why did he say that, Mama?"

I thought about the very tanned white children in Mississippi and wondered how to answer the question. It seemed I had spent my whole life not noticing the color of my skin. Yet now that I had children, it was coming up all the time. But even now, the issue would only be a conscious thought for as long as it took to answer the question. I pondered my answer for a minute. Somewhere in the nooks of my brain, this conversation with my son awakened a memory.

⌘

"There is a new brown girl!" I overheard the statement just before I entered the classroom. It was 1980, and my family had just returned to Uganda from exile in Zambia. My father had returned as soon as the gun smoke had cleared from the overthrow of Idi Amin. He was already very active in the efforts to rebuild the country. I and three of my siblings had returned with our father. The youngest

PATRICIA TIBBS

at the time was now five years old and remained in Zambia with our mother for one extra year because of a contractual commitment that she had with the University of Zambia in Lusaka.

We had lived in Zambia for a little over two years. My father had found employment at the medical school in Lusaka and had sent for the family from Hungary as soon as he was settled. There were several Ugandan families in Zambia at the time. All were families of men who had escaped narrowly from the ruthless reach of Idi Amin. An overwhelming majority were from my father's tribe. I remember wondering who was left to run the country because all these men and women were doctors, lawyers, engineers, pilots, teachers, computer specialists; in short, the sort of people needed to build and run a nation. What saddened me even more later was realizing that those who were in exile at the time were only the tip of the iceberg. Idi Amin had managed to decimate a generation of educated men—men who would not be there to raise their sons, sons who would not reach their full potential because of the absence of their dads. It is estimated that three to five hundred thousand people lost their lives during Idi Amin's reign of terror. This was indeed a tragedy, a tragedy whose full impact has not been measured in any meaningful way because it is more than just numbers of the dead.

⌘

I had never been in a boarding school. When we returned to Uganda, my father had enrolled me in an elite girl's high school run by Franciscan nuns. When I first arrived there with my suitcase, mattress, basin, bucket, and snack box, I could not understand what I was going to do there for three months. I had been told that I would not be allowed to leave the campus for the entire three months. Three months!

I soon found out. The day began with the first bell. There was a mad rush to get a bath in. There was no running water, so each girl collected water in buckets and basins and used the basin to have a bath. Some had electric kettles and could have a hot bath when electricity was available. One learned to clean oneself quite expertly with very little water! Everyone went to breakfast with the next bell. Next

PATRICIA TIBBS

was clean-up time. We all were assigned a chore to do in the morning. These ranged from sweeping the dorms, cleaning the outhouses (there was no running water most of the time), washing dishes in the dining room, or cleaning the shower rooms that did, incidentally, have faucets and shower heads, just no running water. The dorms were at one end of the school and consisted of several large rooms with beds lined up along parallel walls with tiny bedside lockers between each bed. Each room had anywhere from ten to forty girls. The upper class girls in the fifth form had two or three to a room, and the sixth form girls (eighteen and nineteen year olds) had their own rooms.

In Uganda, as in most of Anglophone Africa, schooling consists of seven elementary grades generally completed at age twelve or thirteen. Then one goes on to high school, which consists of four initial or "ordinary level" high school grades, then two "advanced level" high school grades that generally feature American college-level classes. These high school grades are referred to as senior (or form) one, two, three and so forth until form (or senior) six. Most Ugandan children at the time would complete the seven elementary grades, but few would go on to high school, and even fewer would go on to attain the higher school certificate (that is to complete form six). A university education was even rarer. The last time I checked, primary (elementary) school attendance in Uganda was approximately 82 percent, and secondary school attendance was 15 to 20 percent. More boys attended secondary school than girls. This was in the early 2000s. It is probably higher now. But we were the lucky few then. We were truly privileged and blessed to be in that school.

⌘

Assembly followed. There was singing, a prayer, and announcements. Then classes began. With a break midmorning and at lunchtime, classes went on until five o'clock in the evening. There were two hours of free time followed by "prep" time after supper. It was the same for everyone; there were no electives or negotiation. You did what was in the schedule, and it was okay. I could obey rules, and if someone had done it before me, then I could do it too.

PATRICIA TIBBS

Once a month, parents were allowed to visit. Those were much anticipated days. The only way to communicate with our parents was by mail. The postal service was not very reliable, and a letter could take up to three weeks to get to where it needed to go. There was no way to know if your parents would come or not if a letter had not been received in reply, so every girl just hoped. Some large families would bring tons of food and share a picnic with whoever their daughters chose to invite to eat with them. The Muslim families were especially adept at this. There were several such families in this elite catholic school. There could be anywhere from two to five daughters from the same family in the school. They all had the same dad, but their mothers, married to the same man at the same time, were often different. Polygamy was quite common at the time, and still is in the rural areas, and among Muslim families. A few times, one of these Muslim dads who had taken a pilgrimage to Mecca would question me, thinking because of my light brown skin color that I may be Arabian, but they would quickly lose interest when they realized my heritage.

⌘

It was September. School had started one week before, and Chep, one of my friends, was not yet back. There was a rumor around the school and a lot of speculation about the reason for the delay in her return. Could she have gotten married? We were all fifteen years old and were now considered mature and of marriageable age. But we were the lucky ones. We were in an elite boarding school for girls run by nuns. Most of us would graduate from a university. Few would end up married in their teens. We were indeed the lucky ones. But where was Chep?

Chep returned two weeks later, quietly and for the most part unnoticed. This very quiet girl could probably go missing for days before anyone else would notice. But I noticed. I noticed because I had talked to Chep and discovered she had a fascinating mind. The girl knew things about plants and animals that could put a zoologist or botanist to shame. She would have had no trouble identifying every one of my Grandmother Tata's chickens!

I tried to talk to Chep, but something had changed. Something was missing; the animation

PATRICIA TIBBS

was gone. The joy of plants and animals had vanished. I tried to think back to see if I had offended my friend in any way, but I came up blank. After a while, I stopped trying to talk to her. I did have a lot of other friends, after all. But I soon realized that Chep was not talking much to anyone. This really bothered me. Finally one day I found myself in the classroom alone with Chep.

"What is wrong, Chep? You have been very quiet. Is everything okay at home?"

"I am always quiet. Leave me alone."

"See now, I have tried that, but it is not working for me."

I realized then, right in the middle of that conversation, that I really wanted to be a doctor like my father. I had thought about it before, but I had not met any female doctors and was somewhat skeptical about the possibility. It did not matter. My father had told me I could be one if I wanted to, and now I knew that I wanted to. I desperately wanted to see Chep smile again. It was something that went beyond being her friend; it was a calling that grew from that point on. It was the spark that started the flame. I never lost sight of that flame all through medical school when things got really tough.

We were quiet for a long time. I just sat there watching Chep's face as she deliberated what she should say, if anything. I could not at the time fathom what could change a person so dramatically. Little did I know. If I were to guess what could have been wrong with Chep, I would have been so off the mark. I had thought deep enough about it to realize it had to be serious, like maybe she had been raped or forced to marry. But the latter could not be true because she would not have come back at all.

"They came for me in the night," Chep said. "I had refused to have that …that thing done to me. My mother said she was ashamed of me. My father said he would disown me. I did not know where to turn. I had made plans to run away to my godmother's home. She is not of our tribe, and I thought she would understand. They got me that night and took me to that woman's house. They stripped me and held my legs apart. Oh, I screamed. I did not know there was pain such as that. I screamed until I was hoarse. It was over, and I was still screaming. My mother beat me because I had not been tough; my

PATRICIA TIBBS

father spat at me. I bled. Then I was numb. I did not care anymore. I hate my mother. I hate my father..." Chep wept.

I held her for a long time, saying nothing. I could not even begin to imagine this kind of treatment from my father. Your father is supposed to protect you. I supposed that in his own way, Chep's father thought he was doing the best for his daughter. He was, after all, paying a steep price for her education at this school. But how could this be right? There had been some speculation that she had been circumcised, but I did not think it could be true. I had heard about female circumcision but I did not think it was still done anywhere. In 2009, the government of Uganda finally issued an official ban on female genital mutilation, or female circumcision as it is commonly known. It bears no resemblance to male circumcision, which does appear to have some health benefits. Using the word circumcision for female genital mutilation is an attempt to give it some respectability. There is absolutely no point in this atrocious act, which is still practiced to a surprising degree all over the world even though it is now a crime in most countries.

"I still have not had the courage to look at myself down there to see what I look like. I will have to look one day, but all I know is that if I wash too vigorously, there is still pain. It hurt to pee for a long time. That part is better."

Chep was back. Still quiet but in every way Chep.

I never told anyone about what Chep had been through. In time, this quiet girl became a force in the war against female circumcision and told her story many times so that other girls could be protected from this atrocity. Two people discovered their calling on that day. I realized how much I was shielded from because my mother was European. I suspect that my father's education was added protection from the most harmful traditions that many of my friends were exposed to. But protecting children and doing the best for them is what parents do.

⌘

That thought brought me back to my current conundrum. What is the best thing for me to do in this situation with my son? I looked at my son. He

PATRICIA TIBBS

was back to building his spaceship, his plate empty. He had moved on.

I moved on too. In time, he would find his own answers to some of the tough questions. He had sorted the answer to this particular question out in his mind. The fine design of this child's tapestry was beginning to take shape.

Colored

Do Your Best

"That is the bathroom you would use in South Africa!"

I and some friends laughed long and hard. We were tired. We were looking at a magazine picture during a much-needed break in patient care. I looked around me at the amazing representation of God's children in the room. All were doctors, still in training, but we were in the final stretch. All of us would be done with our residency training within the next couple of years and would then be out on our own, making life and death decisions. Most were fathers and mothers, husbands and wives. And as usual in that split instant of race awareness, I took in the beauty of the moment.

There were two white men, one black woman, one Native American woman, and one Asian woman from India. One of the men was deeply tanned, his skin much darker than mine. The other was freckled and fair skinned. The black woman was a deep mahogany, the Native American brown, and the Asian woman was very fair skinned, almost white. Amazing! We had bonded in this place where differences tend to blur and similarities shine out. Everyone was very able and had beaten the odds to be where they were. Each had a long story of the path that had led them to that room. None were like mine, but each one was unique.

I looked again at the magazine picture. It was a picture of a wall with three doors, bathrooms. But instead of "Male," "Female," and "Handicapped," or some such signage, there was "White," "Black," and "Colored." To my colleagues this was an interesting picture, an image to be stored away probably under the title "human interest" or some similar topic. But for me those doors had once conjured up an image that I did not want to replace, and it came back to me vividly.

PATRICIA TIBBS

✽

I stared at the doors with rounded eyes. At fourteen years of age and with an active imagination, I had looked upon these doors and imagined the insides of these rooms. In "White," all the sinks, commodes, and tiles would be white; the floor would be difficult to keep clean, I imagined. In "Black," all the walls would be black, the sinks and commodes too. I wondered if anyone made black commodes. It would have to have good lighting, I imagined. In "Colored," well, there would be none of the problems experienced in the other bathrooms. The floor would be brownish cream, so the dirt would not show; the walls would be a brilliant shine of all the colors of the rainbow: yellow, green, blue, indigo, red, orange, violet, and all the shades in between. Each commode would be a different color. Did they make red sinks? No matter. In my mind, they existed. Each sink would match a commode. I did not go in there, so the image stayed with me.

⌘

"What will they come up with next?"

I brought myself back to the present. It was only ten in the morning, and I was tired. But I was braced and ready as usual for a long day and night of work. It was my turn to take call. My baby had been up a lot the night before, and my husband and I had slept in shifts.

The day had started at five in the morning when my alarm went off. My husband and the baby were curled up in the bed next to me. Our infant girl lay in a perfect curl around my husband's head. A little foot was propped over his neck just below his Adam's apple; the other foot I could not see. Chubby cheeks lay against his bald head with one hand over his eye. I wondered how he could still be asleep, but they were both tired. I kissed them both and tiptoed out of the room. I had just enough time to grab a shower and run out to start my thirty-minute commute to work from the suburbs into the city. At that time of the day, it would be thirty minutes. Any later and I would be stuck in traffic for over one hour.

PATRICIA TIBBS

I had tried to use the available public transit system, but this had not worked well. It never ran at the times I needed it, and I would have to take a bus and transfer to a train. The main problem was I kept falling asleep and missing my stop! As long as I was doing something, whether physical or mental, I was fine. But if I got still for more than a few minutes, I would be asleep before I knew it. I knew that my body was just doing what it needed to do, but it was very inconvenient to wake up and find the bus at the end of its route, eight stops ahead of where I needed to be!

So I drove every day. I had an exciting book I was listening to. I had considerably enriched my knowledge of the classics this way. Almost all my continuing medical education was achieved on my drives. It was convenient, and it meant that I would have more free time with my family that would otherwise be occupied with study.

At six thirty, I reported to the neonatal unit and logged onto the computer to retrieve current labs and medications for my patients. I then began my systematic rounding, which involved getting an update from the nurse about the previous night, scanning the patient nurse notes, and finally examining the baby.

I looked at my first little patient; he was about two pounds in weight and less than a week old. So tiny. He had been born three months early and was clinging to life by a tenuous thread. He was almost invisible in the tangle of monitors and tubes. I looked at him briefly, wondering what life would be like for him if he lived. The odds were overwhelmingly against him. A life of disability, both physical and mental, loomed large before him. But there were many, many stories of wonderful miracles even for children as small as he. My job that day was to make decisions for this child that would bring about the best possible outcome for his future.

I went into "the zone." This is a place in my mind that I go into that allows me to do my job. Here, I can make decisions without the emotional baggage that could cloud my ability to think clearly. I know that my compassionate nature would not allow me to completely detach myself from the reality of the situation. I always operate from a standpoint of "If this was my child…" I know I do this,

PATRICIA TIBBS

but it is never a conscious thought, not when I am in "the zone."

My rounds were interrupted by several monitor alarms going off simultaneously with a nurse's call for help. An infant in a nearby infant warmer was in trouble. He was even smaller than my patient and had not been doing so well in the last few hours. I rushed over to the bedside and made a split-second analysis of the situation. The infant looked dusky, and the monitors showed his oxygen saturation was dropping rapidly. His heart rate also began to drop as I watched. I was the most senior doctor there so I took control. In a rapid series of actions that came from a lot of practice and training, I sounded off instructions, suctioned and adjusted tubing, and pulled out and replaced the tracheal tube. One of the other resident doctors began chest compressions on my cue; I called for medicine, which was administered. All this was happening almost simultaneously.

After a few minutes, I knew then, deep in my heart that we would not save this child that day. The problem was not due to equipment failure, and it was not primarily his heart or his lungs. He had

had a massive brain bleed. Intra-ventricular hemor-rhage! One of the most dreaded complications of being born prematurely.

I continued to work with him, following all the protocols, willing him to live. I was soon joined by the attending physician, a seasoned neonatologist who continued to lead the attempts at reviving the baby. Forty minutes later I looked at his still body. All the tubes had been removed. He looked peace-ful. There had been no peace since he was born. He had been poked and prodded, constantly monitored. He had been attached to so much equipment that he had never been rocked. He had never been held in his mother's arms, had never been held to her soft bosom.

He was now. His mother shed silent tears and lay his still warm body over aching breasts that still filled with milk. She prayed over him and stayed with him for over an hour.

I watched all this quietly with a sore place in my heart. I had come out of "the zone" and just stood there with the grieving woman. There was work to be done, but it could wait. This was where I needed to be right now. There were no words to

PATRICIA TIBBS

say. I hugged her and watched the retreating back of a beaten human being as she left. Where was this child's father? Where was the family? Where was the clan? This should never be dealt with alone!

I was angry, and I was sad. I was not angry or sad because I thought I had failed. No, I had not failed. I had done my best, but ultimately I know that life is not mine to give or take away. I will always do my best. I have heard people say, "Well, your best was not good enough." That is ridiculous. The best is what people have to give. If everyone gave their best, the world would be a very peaceful place indeed. I was angry and sad because this woman was alone.

Alone. The baby's father had not done his best. The baby's family had not done their best for his mother. I thought about my mother and father, my brothers, sisters, and the multiple cousins I have, both Hungarian and Ugandan. I prayed then for my family, and I prayed for this woman. I prayed for a family that was scattered all over the globe that they would never feel as alone as this woman did, even if they happened to be physically alone. There is being alone, as in "my family is on the way," and there is being alone, as in "no one cares."

I turned back to my work and in seconds was back in "the zone." I completed my rounds and had a brief break where pleasant camaraderie was the norm as it had been that morning. Rounds with the attending physician ensued, during which time plans for each infant were confirmed. I left the rounds many times to answer a page from nurses, other doctors, other hospitals, the pharmacy, or the lab. This would happen multiple times through the day.

It was fascinating to see how each individual doctor handled this situation of being on call. Some would begin the day with a cordial response to each query and end it sounding like a raving lunatic, yelling at whoever happened to be close by. Some began the day like that! I believe that it was only partly due to the program itself. Yes, it was intense. Yes, it was emotionally and physically taxing, but I had seen doctors who had done just fine, always treating everyone with respect and apologizing when they failed. It seems to have everything to do with where one's strength comes from. One needed a deep well

PATRICIA TIBBS

from which to draw. I thought of the well in my grandmother's yard in Hungary. It was deep. One could not see the bottom, yet every time the bucket went down, clean water came up. But you had to go deep enough.

Everybody has a well from which to draw. The well starts off with clean, clear water. It stays that way if it is appropriately sheltered, and as long as you do not throw trash into it. Some people have so much trash in their wells that there isn't even water to draw. This is fixable. It takes work and some help from others, and from God. I remember times in my life when my well has been murky indeed. I was a raving nut by the end of the day. I have long realized that I would need to constantly keep my well clean because I needed to draw deep from it often. I wanted that water to be crystal clear as much as it depended on me. Wells sometimes begin to produce dirty water as a function of their location and geography. It is then time to move the well. There is no point staying in a job if you do not like it. If the circumstances are such that you cannot move, clean up your well and change your attitude. Life is too short to waste complaining and doing a job badly because you do not like it. I have been amazed at how one's outlook on life changes when one realizes how unique one is, how God gave each one of us a set of gifts and a work to do.

Over the years, I have wondered sometimes why some people chose to be what they are if they appear to hate it so much. Many of those just needed to clean up their wells; deal with emotional baggage at home; do their best for God, for their families, and for themselves. Only then can they give their best to others. When your well is cleaned up, only then can you see clearly to that place where you need to be. That job, that calling, which is so uniquely "you" that no one else on the planet could do it but you.

I spent the afternoon doing procedures that needed to be done but were not urgent. Then it was time to receive "sign-out" from everyone who was going home that day. I and my team would spend the night in the residents' lounge, ready and accessible for any emergency that would come up.

   PATRICIA TIBBS

⌘

I was called to attend a caesarian section delivery. I scrubbed up and put on sterile attire to go into the operating room. It was full of state-of-the-art equipment, lights, steel, and chrome. Sterile. The mother was lying on the operating table awake and talking. Her upper torso, head, and her husband were separated from the surgery site by a blue sterile drape. She was numbed up by spinal anesthesia from her chest down. The obstetrician was teasing, some inside joke. There was free banter. The surgery began, and it got quiet. Then the miracle of birth! The baby did not cry initially and seemed floppy and weak.

There was momentary panic and then "the zone." I took the baby from the Obstetrician quickly, laying him on the warmed infant warmer. I suctioned his airway quickly while the nurse I was with dried him off and rubbed his back to stimulate him. I started bag and mask ventilation, and seconds later there was a deep breath and a loud gusty cry. The emergency was over. The baby was nice and pink and kicking for all he was worth. Conversa-

tion resumed. I continued to watch the baby closely, monitoring his breathing and heart rates while the nurse foot-printed, tagged, and cleaned him up. I could not help contrasting this situation with a time in my past.

⌘

It was 1990. The war in the north of Uganda was ongoing and had left its mark on the town that had been deserted when evidence of fighting had come close, but now people were returning. The LORD's Resistance Army (LRA) led by Joseph Kony had caused havoc in the North of Uganda. This war led by a ruthless maniac resulted in over one million people being displaced at the peak of the war. Mr. Kony claimed he wanted to take over Uganda and run it biblically by the Ten Commandments. The worst effects of this war were the abduction of children. Many of these children were forced to watch the murder of their parents, and then the girls became sex slaves, and the boys were forced to become child soldiers. People would flee into the bushes, away from their homes when they heard

PATRICIA TIBBS

that 'Kony' was coming. These rebels would raid villages, plundering the homes and people, killing many, capturing the rest and leave a path of death as they moved from one area to the next.

I had travelled there to check on my aunts and cousins and also to check on the homestead. My Grandmother, Tata, had been dead for over five years, but my father maintained the farm and home-stead, building some more permanent buildings. I was with my cousin, who was also checking on the family. We were both interns and had gone through medical school together. While we were resting at my uncle's home, a man rode up on a bicycle, frantic because his wife was dying. The woman had been in labor for two days and had not had the baby. She was weak and had become very still. I looked at my cousin. We were not quite ready to be independent doctors yet, but we were all the woman had. I was very reluctant. But even as I acknowledged my feel-ing of inadequacy in this situation, I knew what we had to do. The woman's husband was uttering loud praise to God for his wife's salvation in the form of the "brown" doctor. Little did he know that my very Ugandan and dark-skinned cousin was the smarter of the two of us, and probably a better surgeon. I thanked God many times that I was indeed a half decent doctor because I was often elevated to a pedestal that I could only hope to live up to in the poverty-stricken villages in Uganda. We got into the car and drove to the hospital. There were some patients milling about, but otherwise it looked like a bunch of ghost buildings.

The hospital consisted of several independent buildings, brick and iron roofed each with its own function. We walked past the men's ward and were led to the labor ward. There were a few people around, but the place was generally deserted as far as hospitals went. There were no beds, all had been looted, and there was nothing, not even the window panes. The wind blew in freely. The buildings still stood and would one day hum again with hospital noises, but for now all we could hear was a woman's wailing, with some other sobbing sounds in the background. At first, we thought the woman had died, but it was her mother so distraught by the thought of the loss of yet another daughter.

My cousin roused us all into action. While the man rebuked his mother-in-law not to cry until all

PATRICIA TIBBS

was lost, I did a quick exam of the woman, who was exhausted and dehydrated but still conscious. The head of the baby was in her left flank. She would never be able to deliver this baby naturally. She would die if someone did not perform a caesarian section and take the baby out. We ran to what used to be the operating room. It was a shambles. We looked around—nothing there but the operating table that had presumably been too heavy to lift. We doubled back, running into an elderly nurse wearing an old but well-pressed and clean nurse's uniform. She had come out to see what the ruckus was about. Quickly the situation was explained to her. The nurse had some supplies that might be helpful but was hesitant to give them out. My cousin and I understood immediately, even though we were irritated by her stance. No questions were asked, and there was no arrogant analysis of the nurse's unwillingness to help. This was war, and the nurse had a family to feed. Maybe later we could analyze her unwillingness to help in this situation, but we were not in her shoes. We did not know what she herself had been through in this war. Right now, we needed to do our best for the dying woman, not argue about the merits of a benevolent spirit. Between the two of us, we came up with some money to pay for supplies.

I stared at our "supplies": two pairs of surgical gloves, the thick old kind, not in any kind of wrapping; two small packages of catgut suture and one of silk; a blade; two random forceps; a curved surgical needle; some cotton wool; and a small bottle of ether. The family's meal was cooking on a nearby makeshift stove. The food was removed, and all our equipment was boiled for several minutes.

"You are anesthesia. I am the surgeon." My cousin ordered me to the head of the patient. We had fire heated a metal tray; that was the sterile zone. My cousin washed her hands several times with soap and water, and she washed the woman's belly several times also with soap and water. We hoped it would be enough. We both donned gloves; we were as ready as we were ever going to be. The family had been ordered out but was now looking in through the window.

I thought back to the pharmacological properties of ether. I could monitor my patient very crudely but effectively by keeping an eye on the

PATRICIA TIBBS

heart rate and the pupils of her eyes. I soaked the cotton with ether and laid it over the patient's nose. A brief coughing episode, and within minutes, the patient was asleep. I gave the sign; my cousin began. We had both done many cesarean sections already, but never like this. We had always had a senior doctor with us or close by until then.

My cousin was quick. A classical cut, and minutes later, the baby came into view. With some difficulty, the baby was extracted. He was floppy, and I could detect no heartbeat. I rubbed him and held him at an angle to let any fluids out. He was dead. I wondered later if he could have survived if I had suction equipment, oxygen, and a bag and mask. I did not dwell on it then. I had done my best, which was what I had to give. The mother was alive and had other children to nurture. I continued to monitor the woman until my cousin was done. By the time the last stitch was in, the woman was almost fully awake and had to be restrained, but I could not risk any more ether. The nurse took over. Nursing in this war zone was familiar to her. Oral fluids would be given, and some antibiotics had been found that were started immediately. Amazingly, the woman survived. I was reminded again how I have no control over life itself. This woman should have died. All we had to do was give our best.

⌘

The nurse was done cleaning and tagging the infant as I came out of my reverie.

I got four good hours of sleep that night. By the time I got home the next day, I was exhausted, but I was at peace. I had done a good day's work, and I had learned some new things. I had a one-hour catnap and went to get our daughter. It was raining, and there was some traffic. While I was at a stop light, the sun came out. A beautiful, brilliant rainbow came into view. I stared at the brilliant colors, beautiful colors. Each color by itself, while beautiful, could not make a rainbow. All the colors side by side, working together, make something worth seeing.

⌘

I thought back on this time. I now have four children, each one weaving the tapestry of their own

PATRICIA TIBBS

lives with the cords my husband and I hand them. I will continue to give my best because I have been given the best. My mother and father, raised very differently, came together and wove something beautiful into six lives. Both my grandmothers are dead now, but they live on in the lives of those who continue to pass down the cords that make life so beautiful.

We have but one life to live. Live it. Tomorrow is uncertain, but I will do my part, leave my mark to make it a better place for my children and grandchildren. I will continue to pass on the best cords I have. The design of the tapestry in at least four lives depends very heavily on me.